What Do You Eat for Lunch?

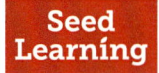

Seed
Learning

sandwich

noodles

chicken

rice

fish

soup

salad

taco

What do you eat for lunch?

I eat a sandwich.

What do you eat for lunch?

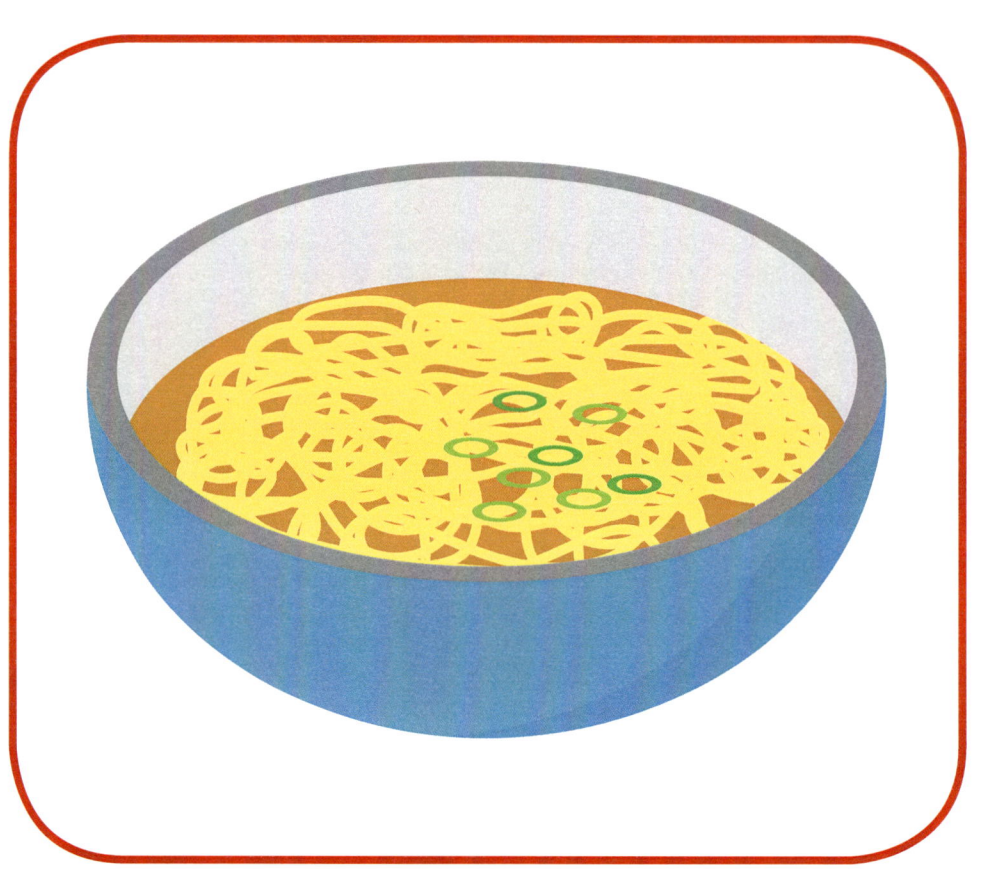

I eat noodles.

What do you eat for lunch?

I eat salad.

What do you eat for lunch?

I eat rice.

What do you eat for lunch?

I eat soup, chicken soup.

Let's learn more about Turkey.

Turkish coffee